Introducing The Positions...

for CELLO—Vol. II

SECOND, SECOND-AND-A-HALF, THIRD AND THIRD-AND-A-HALF POSITIONS

There are many students today, who, after an elementary training in cello playing, restricted entirely to the first position of their instrument, have joined the ranks of school and amateur orchestras. As the real purpose of position playing is to extend the tonal range of the cello, those students who play only in the first position, by necessity, have no alternative than to remain in elementary ensemble groups. They cannot become members of advanced school orchestras or semi-professional groups, because of their inability to play in the higher positions of their instrument. When an attempt is made to study these higher positions, they either find themselves confronted with an array of un-graded technical material, completely inade-quate for their particular needs, or else find that the material to be studied in each of the several positions is not sufficient in quantity in any one book to be of real service to them.

In actuality, there are seven so called "neck" positions on the cello, the first four of which utilize the bass clef, and the last three (fifth, sixth, and seventh) the tenor clef. Beyond the seventh position there exist the "thumb" posi-tions, which are used only in advanced cello playing. The higher positions with which the cellist first should become familiar are the sec-ond, third, and fourth, as the tonal range cov-ered by these positions is quite adequate for playing much of the literature encountered in the orchestra of today.

As Introducing the Positions, for cello, consti-tutes purely an introductory course in position playing, it takes up only the second, third, and fourth positions. Of these positions, the fourth is the most important, and should be studied before the others, as it gives the students, at once, a grasp of the range of the cello most needed. Therefore, Volume One of Introducing the Positions is given over entirely to the fourth position, with shifting from the first to the fourth position, and from the fourth position back to the first position. Volume Two of Introducing the Positions takes up the second position, sec-ond-and-a-half position, third position, and third-and-a-half position, with shifting to and from these various positions.

After students have mastered the material presented in Volumes One and Two of Intro-ducing the Positions for cello, they will have had adequate preparation for going ahead with more advanced work, such as studying the fifth, sixth, and seventh positions, as well as the various thumb positions. For this study, it is recommended that students turn to the tra-ditional technical studies and etudes of cello literature, such as the works of Werner, Kum-mer, Dotzauer, Duport, Schroeder, and Davidoff.

If Introducing the Positions for cello proves itself a boon to those ambitious students in quest of material and procedures that will en-able them to become better performers on their instrument, and thus become qualified for mem-bership in advanced orchestras and ensembles, as well as more proficient in solo playing, the writer will feel gratified to know that his hum-ble efforts have been of some educational sig-nificance.

Harvey S. Whistler, Ph. D.

The Second Position

A String

A STRING FINGERING

PREPARATORY STUDIES

7

8

9

10

11

12

13

D String

PREPARATORY STUDIES

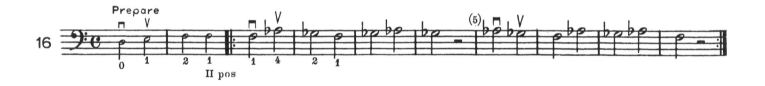

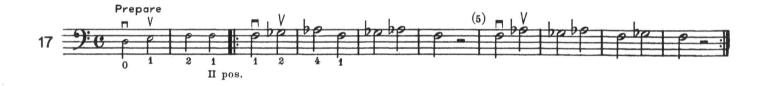

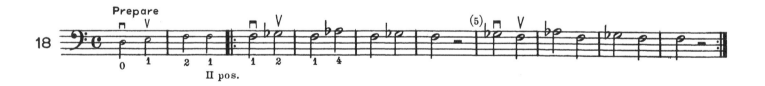

20

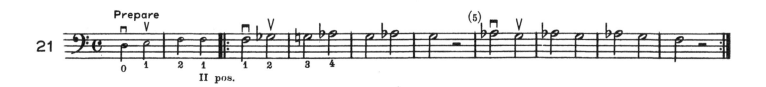

21

22

23

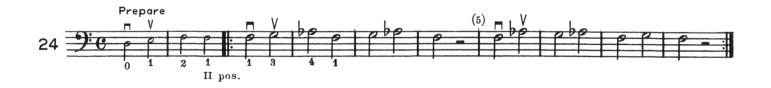

24

25

26

G String

G STRING FINGERING

27

PREPARATORY STUDIES

28

29

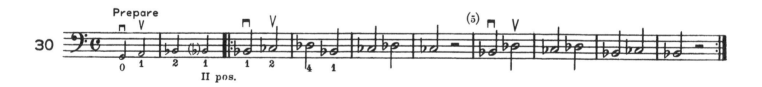

30

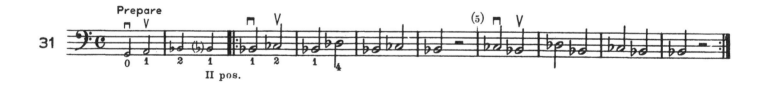

31

32

33

34

35

36

37

38
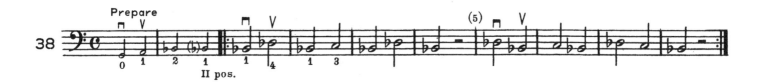

39
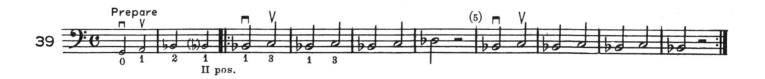

C String

C STRING FINGERING

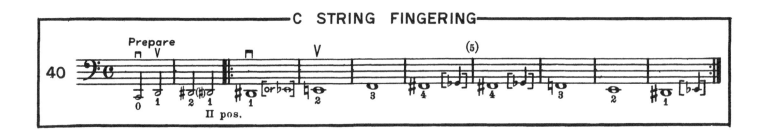

PREPARATORY STUDIES

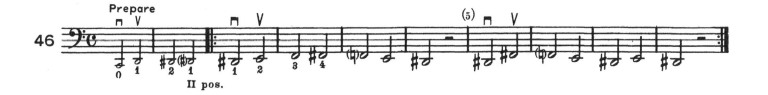

46

47

48

49

50

51

52

Technic Builders in Second Position
A String

Also practice technic builders (1) slurring each two tones, and (2) slurring each complete measure.

Before commencing, prepare for the SECOND POSITION by playing

D String

Before commencing, prepare for the SECOND POSITION by playing

G String

Before commencing, prepare for the SECOND POSITION by playing

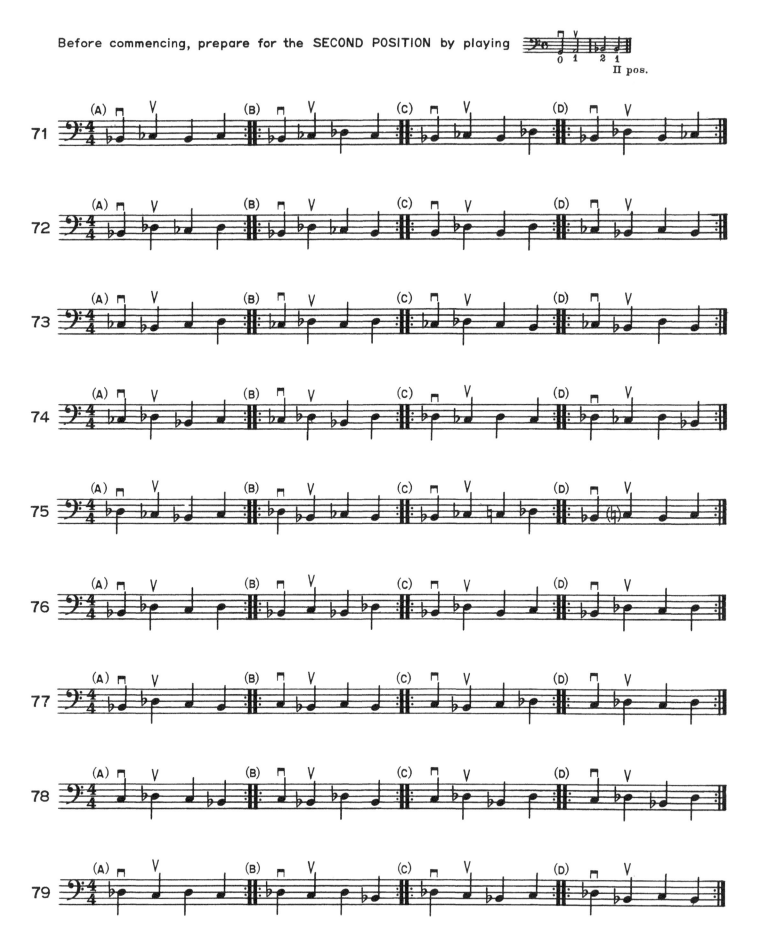

C String

Before commencing, prepare for the SECOND POSITION by playing

Shifting from First to Second Position

When shifting from the first to a higher position, do not take the finger up and put it down again; instead, SLIDE into the higher position.

A STRING

D STRING

G STRING

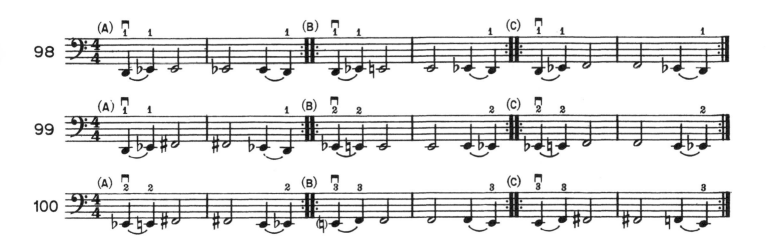

Shifting from One Finger to Another

The student should slide forward on the finger that was last down, and likewise, shift backward on the finger that was last down.

The small note in the following exercises indicates the movement of the finger in shifting, and as the student perfects his ability to shift from one note to another, the small note eventually should not be heard.

Lowered Form of Second Position
A String

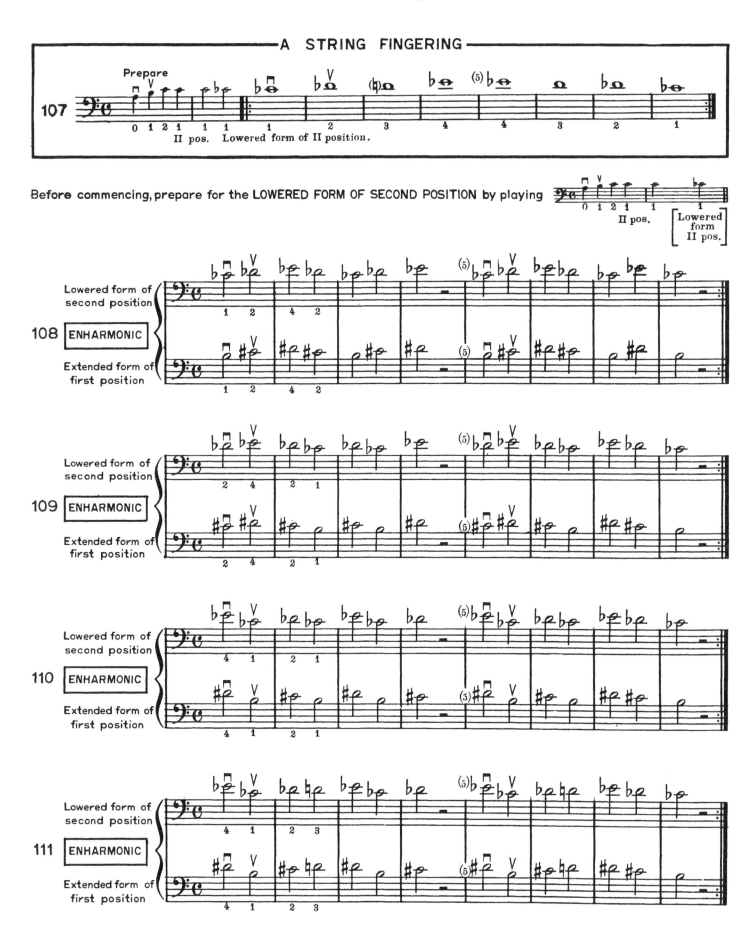

Before commencing, prepare for the LOWERED FORM OF SECOND POSITION by playing

D String

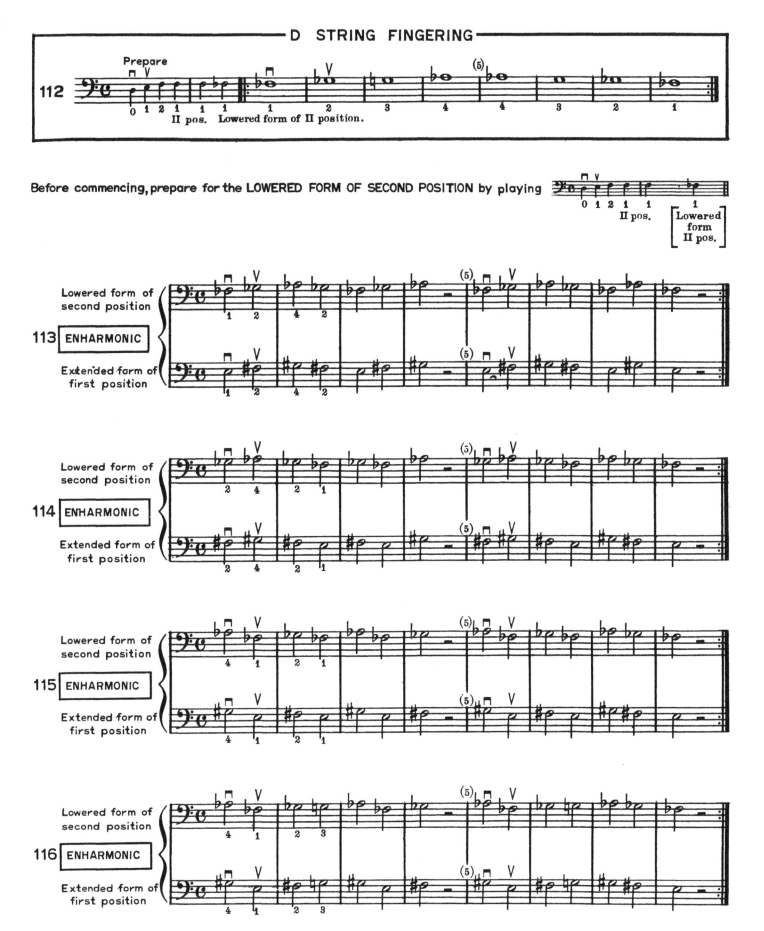

G String

Before commencing, prepare for the LOWERED FORM OF SECOND POSITION by playing

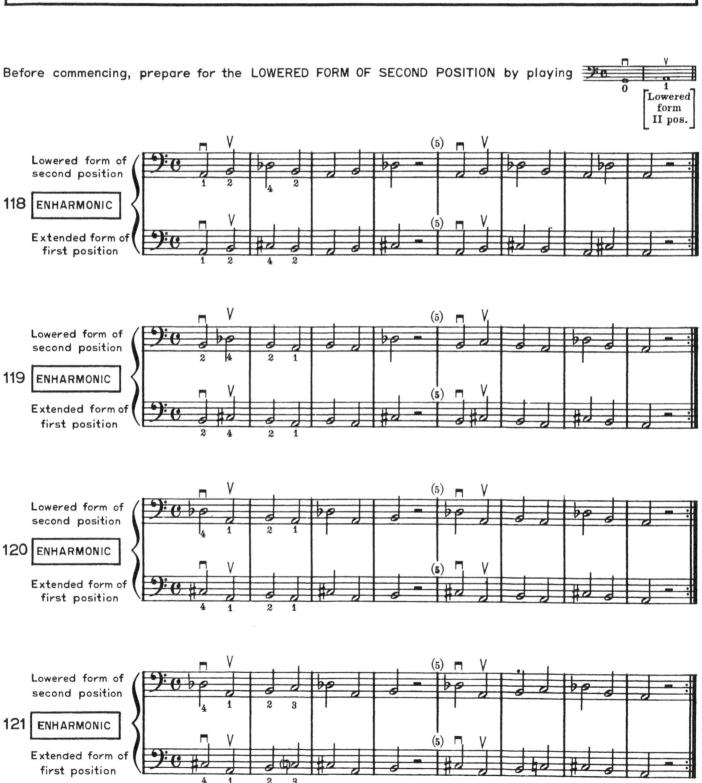

C String

Before commencing, prepare for the LOWERED FORM OF SECOND POSITION by playing

Extended Form of Second Position

A String

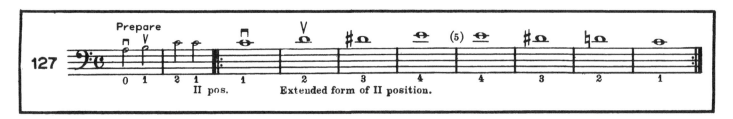

127

Prepare

0 1 2 1
II pos. 1 2 3 4 4 3 2 1
Extended form of II position.

Before commencing, prepare for the EXTENDED FORM OF SECOND POSITION by playing

0 1 2 1
II pos.

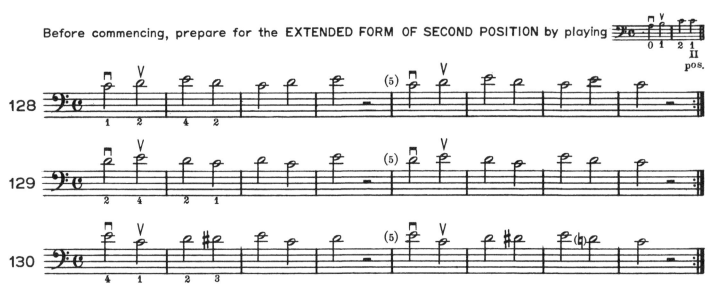

128

1 2 4 2 (5)

129

2 4 2 1 (5)

130

4 1 2 3 (5)

D String

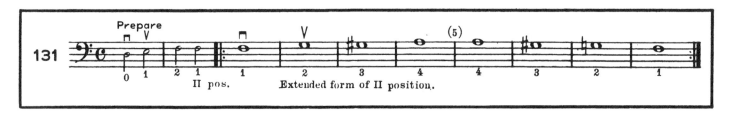

131

Prepare

0 1 2 1
II pos. 1 2 3 4 4 3 2 1 (5)
Extended form of II position.

Before commencing, prepare for the EXTENDED FORM OF SECOND POSITION by playing

0 1 2 1
II pos.

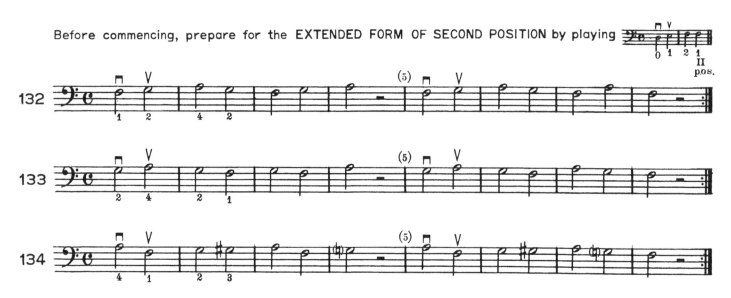

132

1 2 4 2 (5)

133

2 4 2 1 (5)

134

4 1 2 3 (5)

20

G String

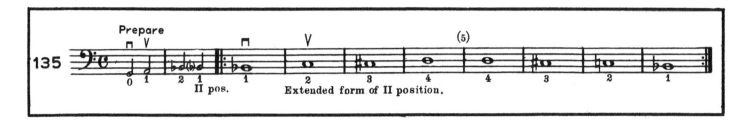

Before commencing, prepare for the EXTENDED FORM OF SECOND POSITION by playing

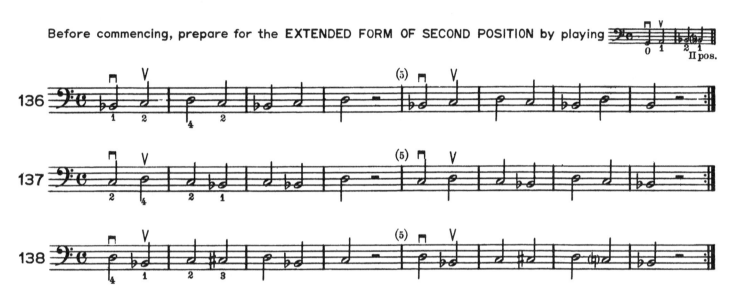

C String

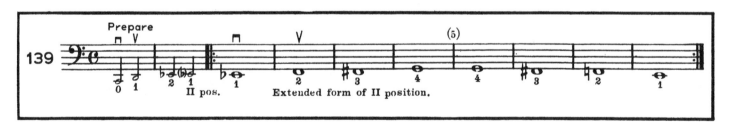

Before commencing, prepare for the EXTENDED FORM OF SECOND POSITION by playing

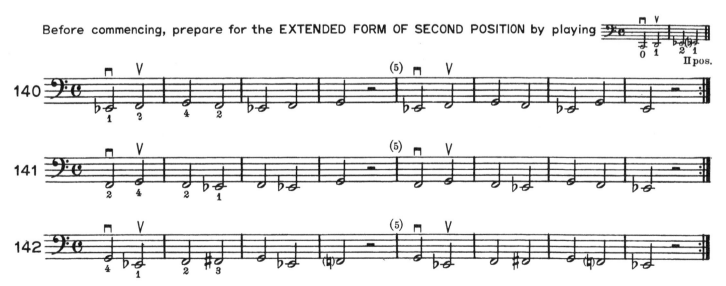

Second Position Etude No. 1

WERNER

(Remain in Second Position throughout.)

Second Position Etude No. 2

DUPORT

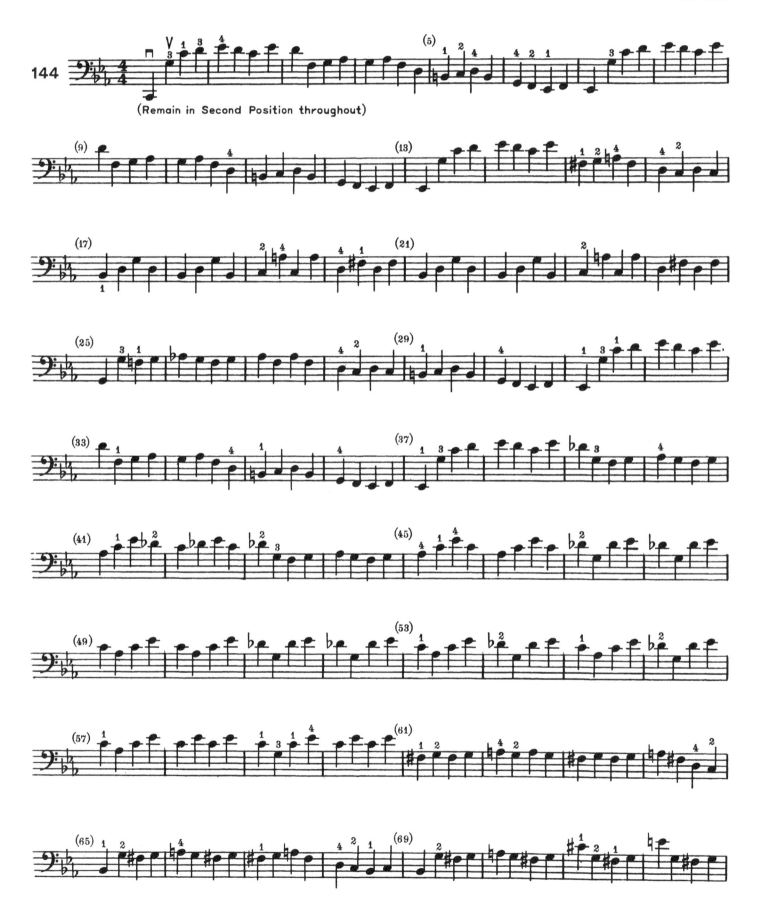

(Remain in Second Position throughout)

The Second-and-a-Half Position

(One-half tone higher than regular Second Position)

A String

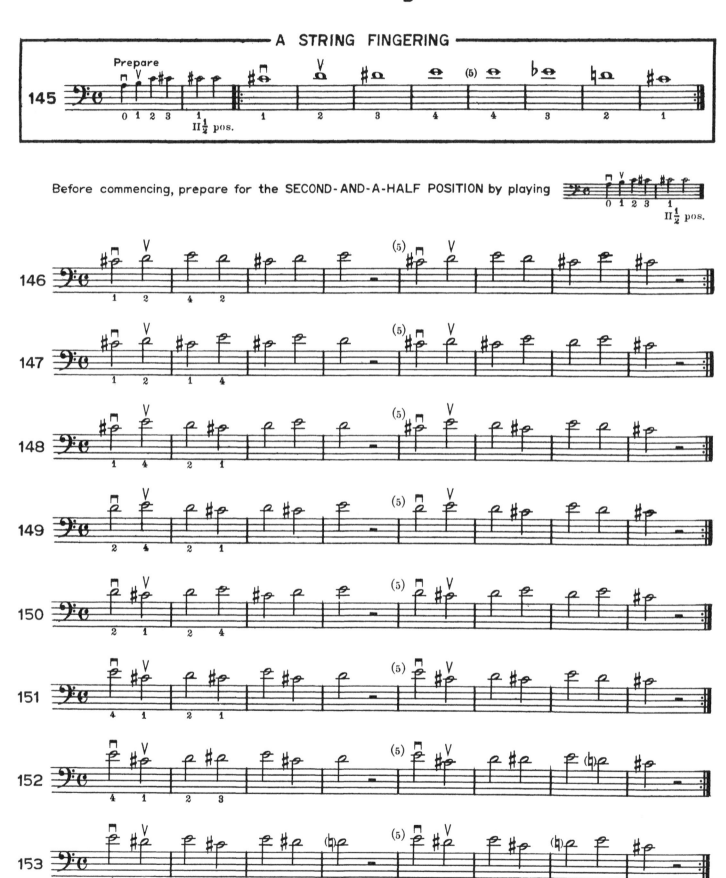

D String

D STRING FINGERING

154

Before commencing, prepare for the SECOND-AND-A-HALF POSITION by playing

155

156

157

158

159

160

161

162

G String

Before commencing, prepare for the SECOND-AND-A-HALF POSITION by playing

C String

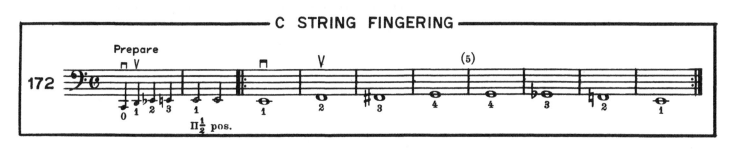

Before commencing, prepare for the SECOND-AND-A-HALF POSITION by playing

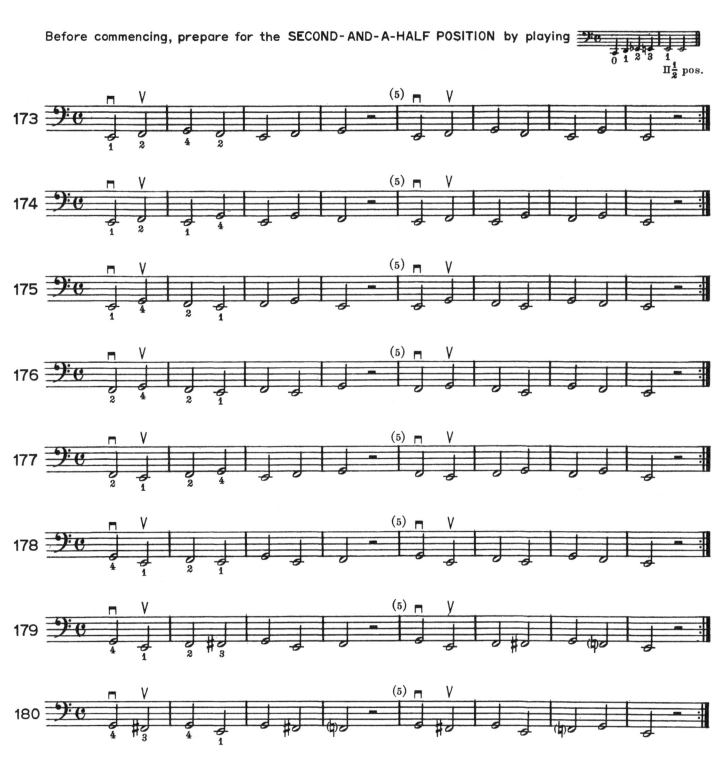

Shifting from First to Second-and-a-Half Position

The student must remember to shift forward on the finger that was last down, and likewise, shift backward on the finger that was last down.

The student also must remember that the small note in the following exercises merely indicates the movement of the finger in shifting, and as the ability to shift from one note to another is perfected, the small note eventually must not be heard.

Chromatic Scale

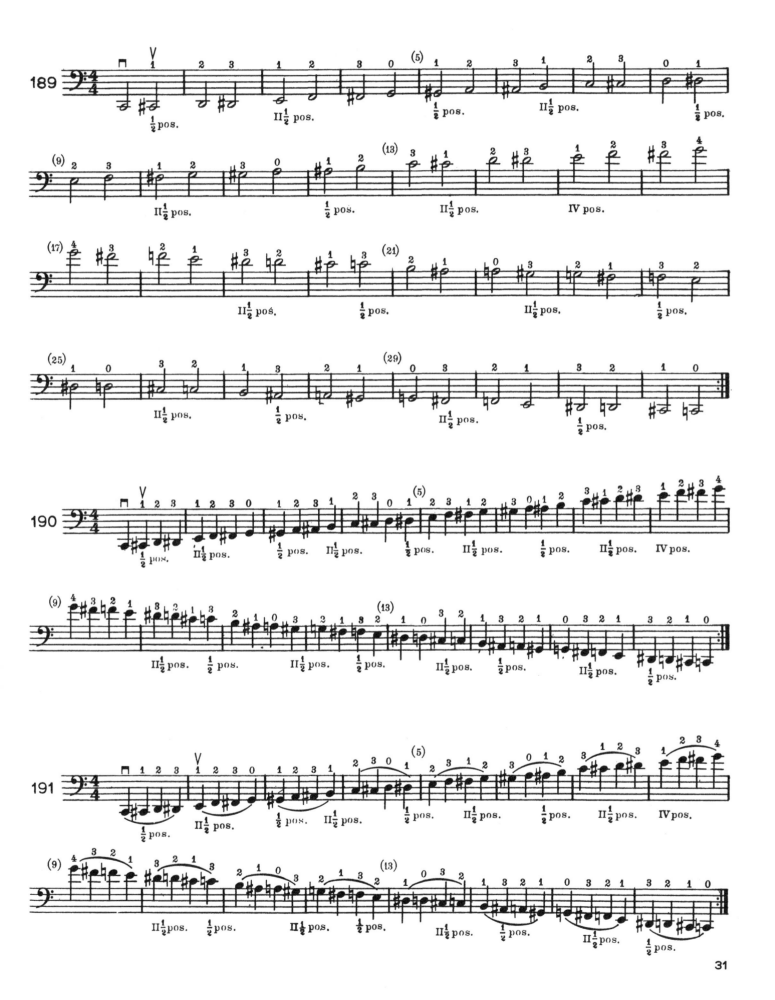

The Third Position

A String

A STRING FINGERING

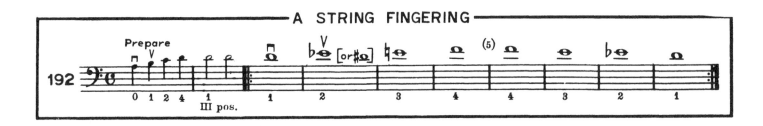

PREPARATORY STUDIES

198

199

200

201

202

203

204

D String

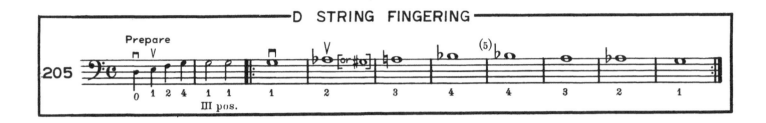

D STRING FINGERING

205

PREPARATORY STUDIES

206

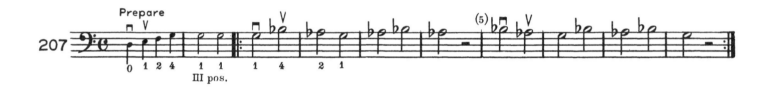

207

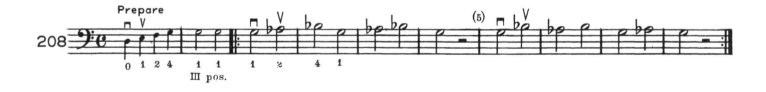

208

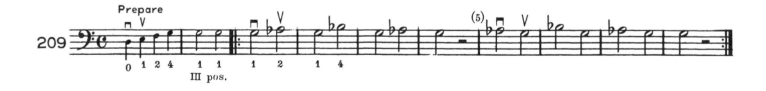

209

210

211

212

213

214

215

216

217

G String

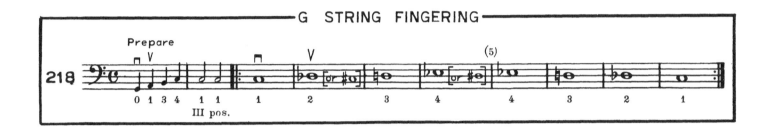

PREPARATORY STUDIES

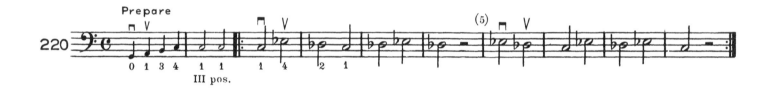

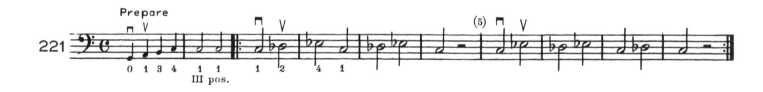

36

C String

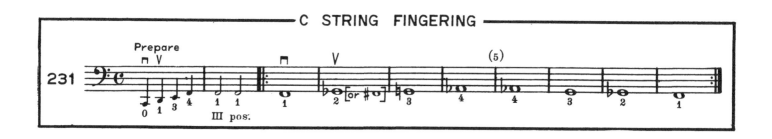

PREPARATORY STUDIES

237

238

239

240

241

242

243

Technic Builders in Third Position
A String

Also practice technic builders (1) slurring each two tones, and (2) slurring each complete measure.

Before commencing, prepare for the THIRD POSITION by playing

D String

Before commencing, prepare for the THIRD POSITION by playing

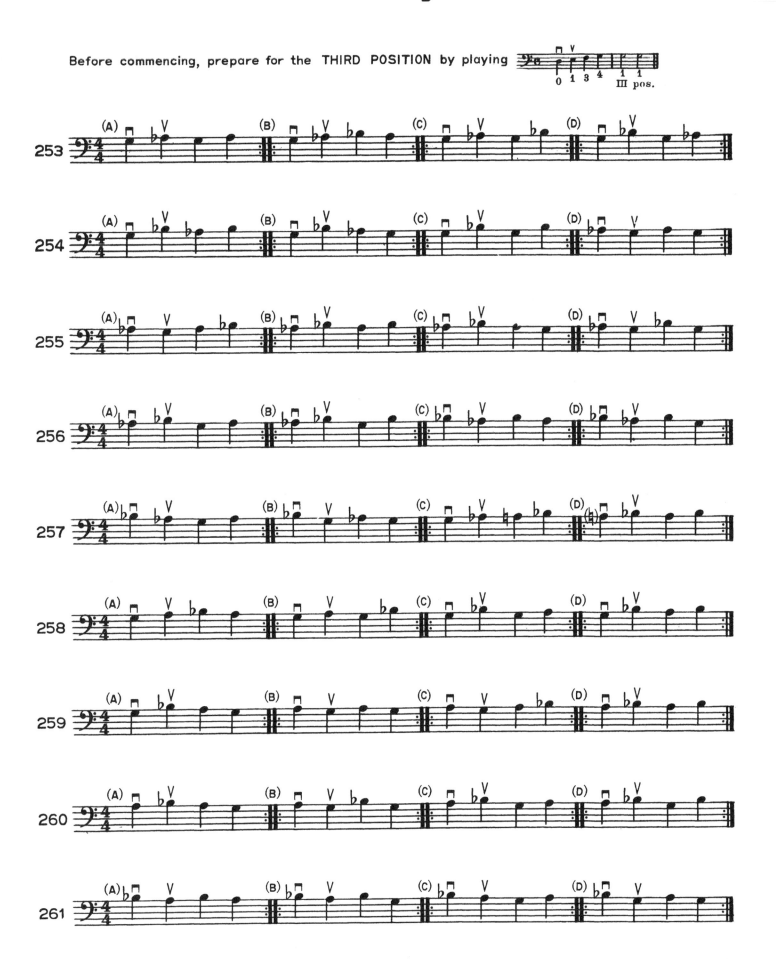

G String

Before commencing, prepare for the THIRD POSITION by playing

262

263

264

265

266

267

268

269

270

C String

Before commencing, prepare for the THIRD POSITION by playing

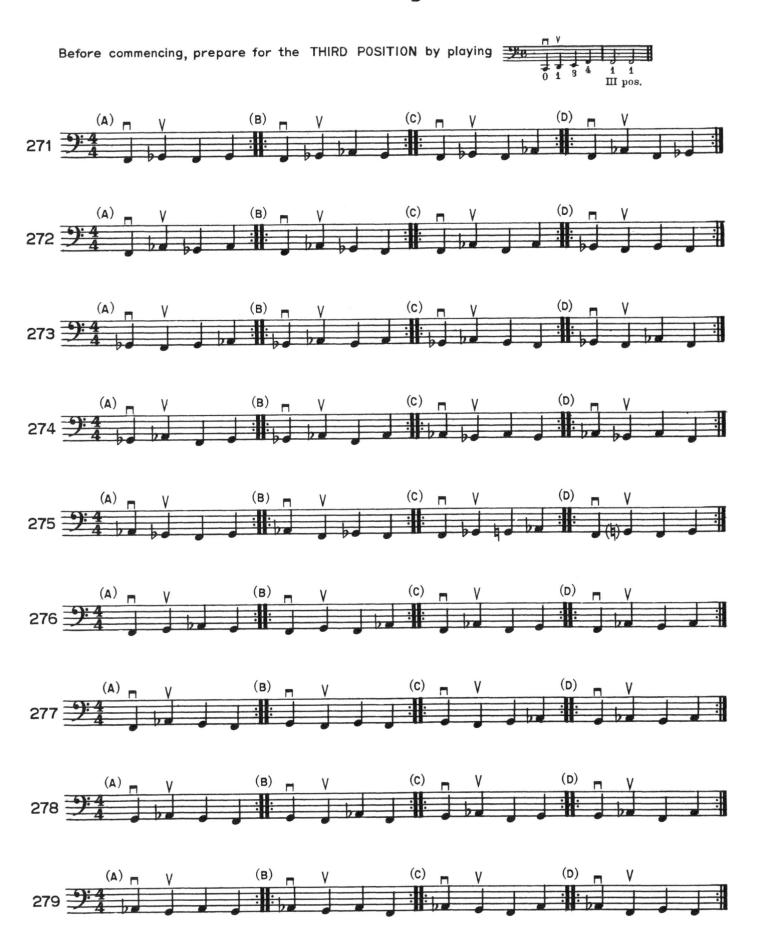

Shifting from First to Third Position

When shifting from the first to a higher position, do not take the finger up and put it down again; instead, SLIDE into the higher position.

C STRING

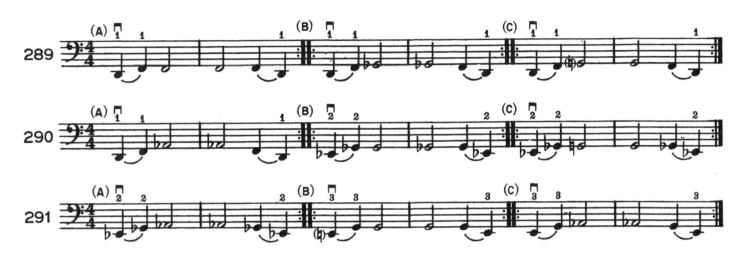

Shifting from One Finger to Another

The student should slide forward on the finger that was last down, and likewise, shift backward on the finger that was last down.

The small note in the following exercises indicates the movement of the finger in shifting, and as the student perfects his ability to shift from one note to another, the small note eventually should not be heard.

Lowered Form of Third Position

A String

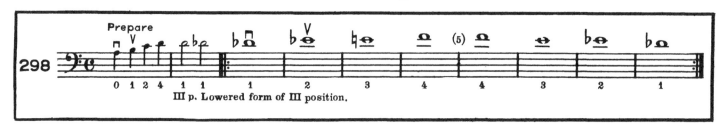

Before commencing, prepare for the LOWERED FORM OF THIRD POSITION by playing

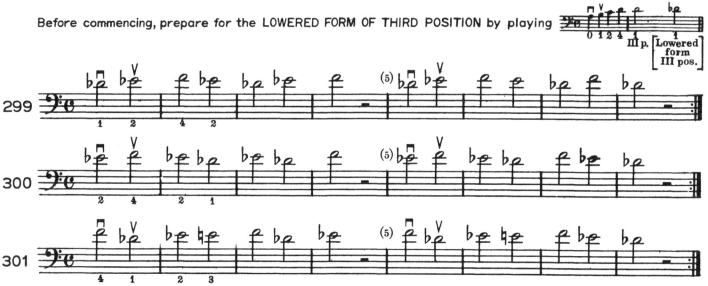

D String

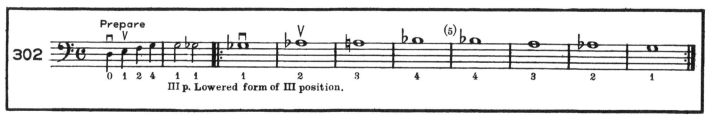

Before commencing, prepare for the LOWERED FORM OF THIRD POSITION by playing

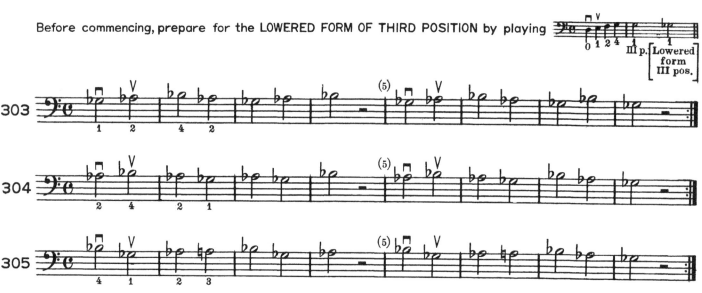

G String

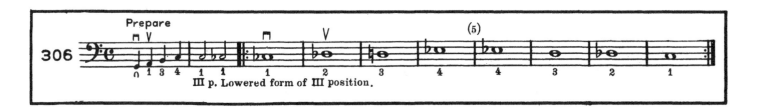

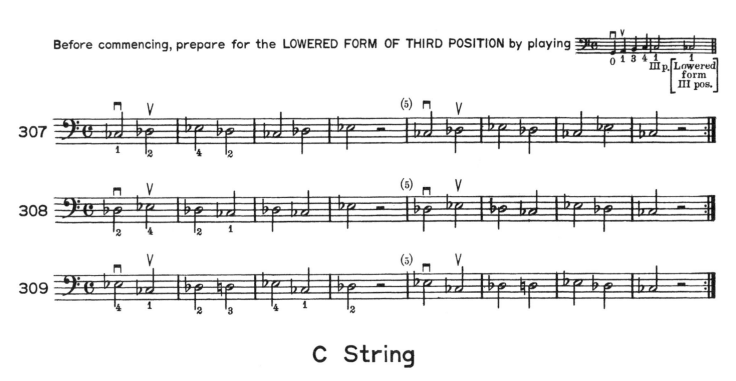

Before commencing, prepare for the LOWERED FORM OF THIRD POSITION by playing

C String

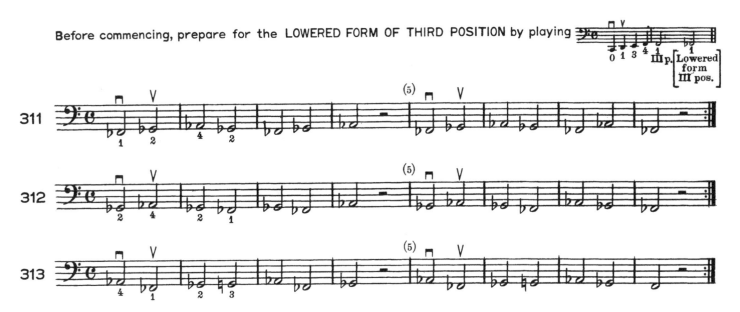

Before commencing, prepare for the LOWERED FORM OF THIRD POSITION by playing

Extended Form of Third Position

A String

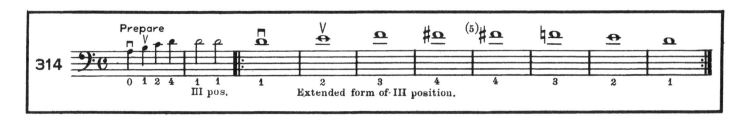

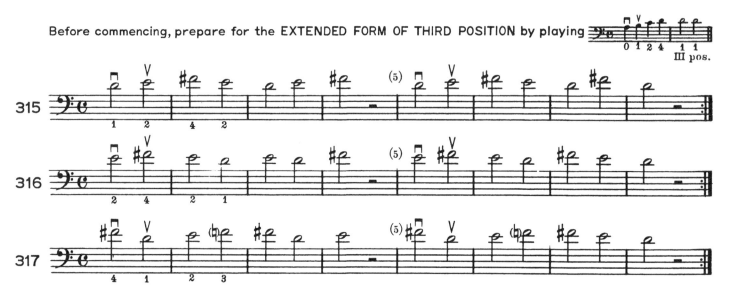

D String

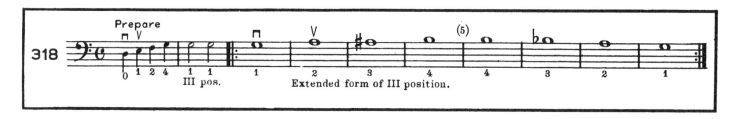

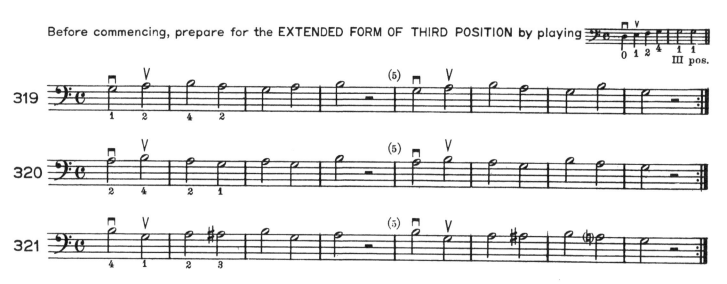

G String

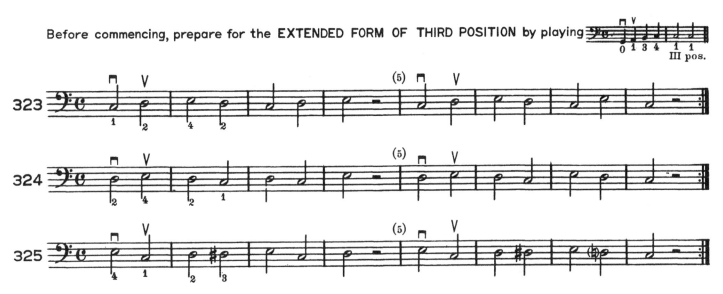

Before commencing, prepare for the EXTENDED FORM OF THIRD POSITION by playing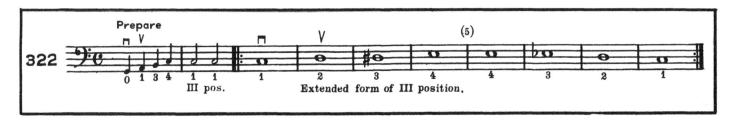

C String

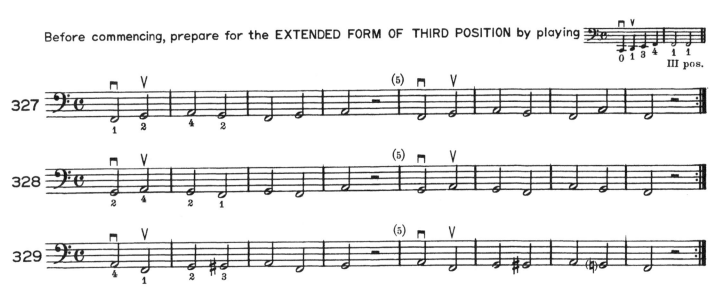

Before commencing, prepare for the EXTENDED FORM OF THIRD POSITION by playing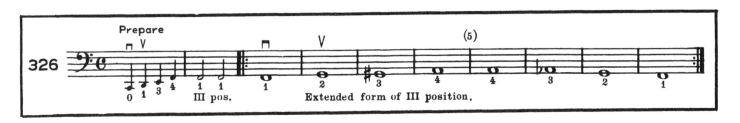

Third Position Etude

WERNER

51

Shifting Etude

(Through Four Positions)

DUPORT

The Third-and-a-Half Position

(One-half tone higher than regular Third Position)

A String

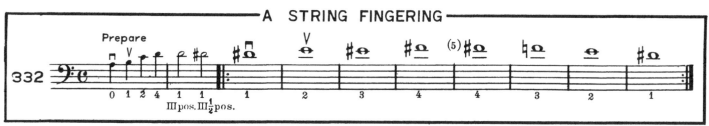

Before commencing, prepare for the THIRD-AND-A-HALF POSITION by playing

D String

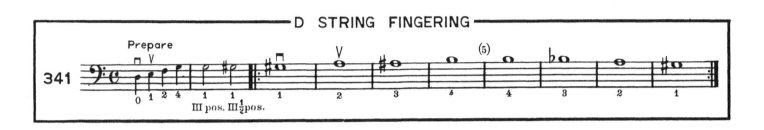

Before commencing, prepare for the THIRD-AND-A-HALF POSITION by playing

G String

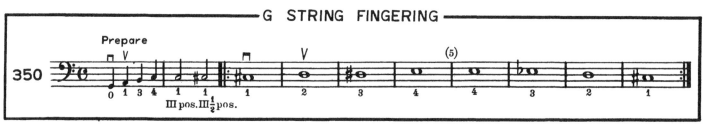

Before commencing, prepare for the THIRD-AND-A-HALF POSITION by playing

C String

Before commencing, prepare for the THIRD-AND-A-HALF POSITION by playing

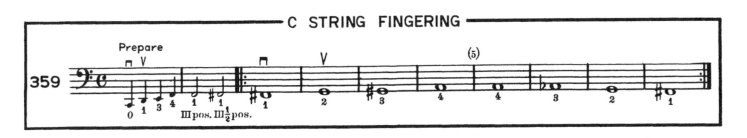

Shifting from First to Third-and-a-Half Position

The student must remember to shift forward on the finger that was last down, and like-wise, shift backward on the finger that was last down.

The student also must remember that the small note in the following exercises merely indicates the movement of the finger in shifting, and as the ability to shift from one note to another is perfected, the small note eventually must not be heard.

Scale of E Major

(Employing the Second-and-a-Half and the Third-and-a-Half Positions)

Before commencing, prepare for the Second-and-a-Half Position by playing

Exercises in Harmonics

A STRING

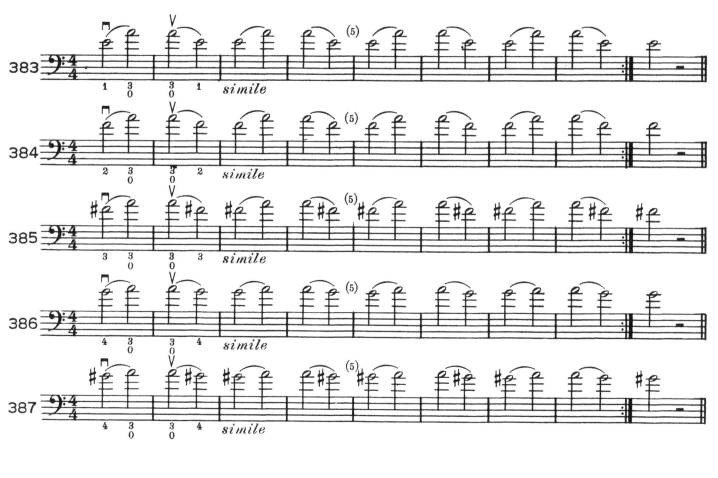

D STRING

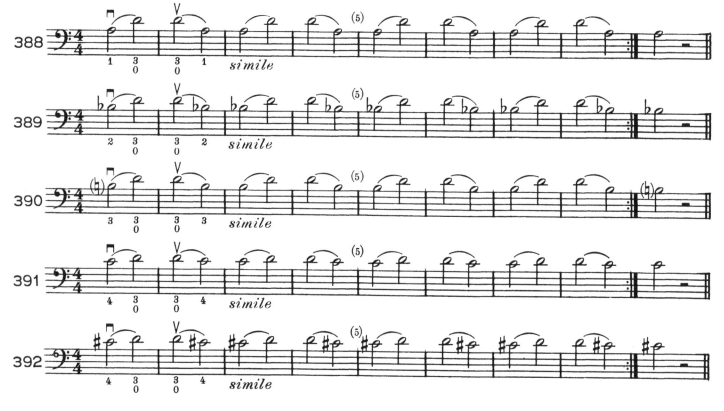

G STRING

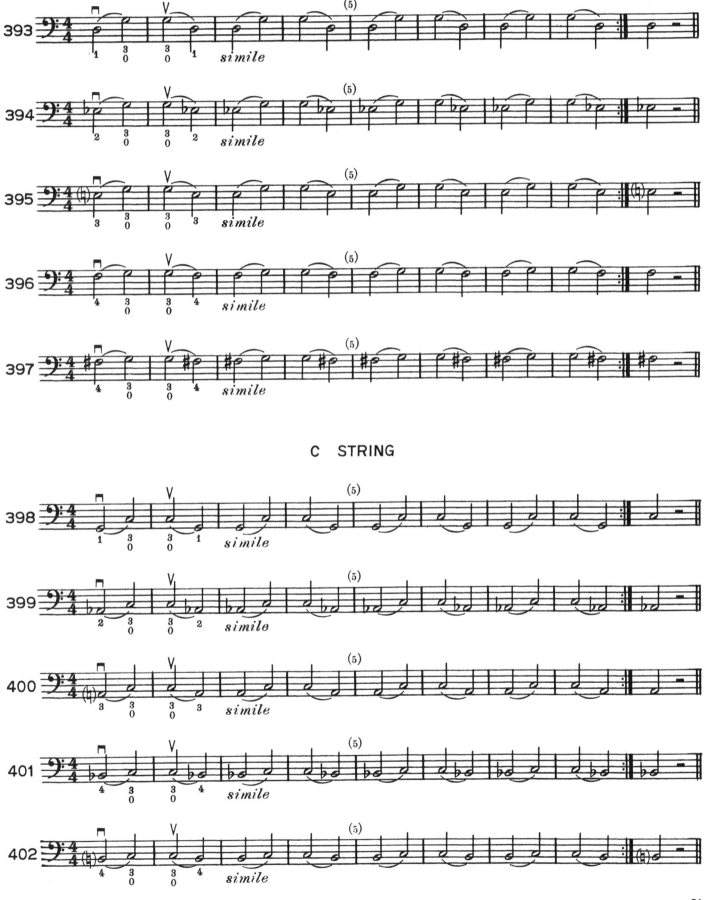

C STRING

Advanced Exercises in Harmonics

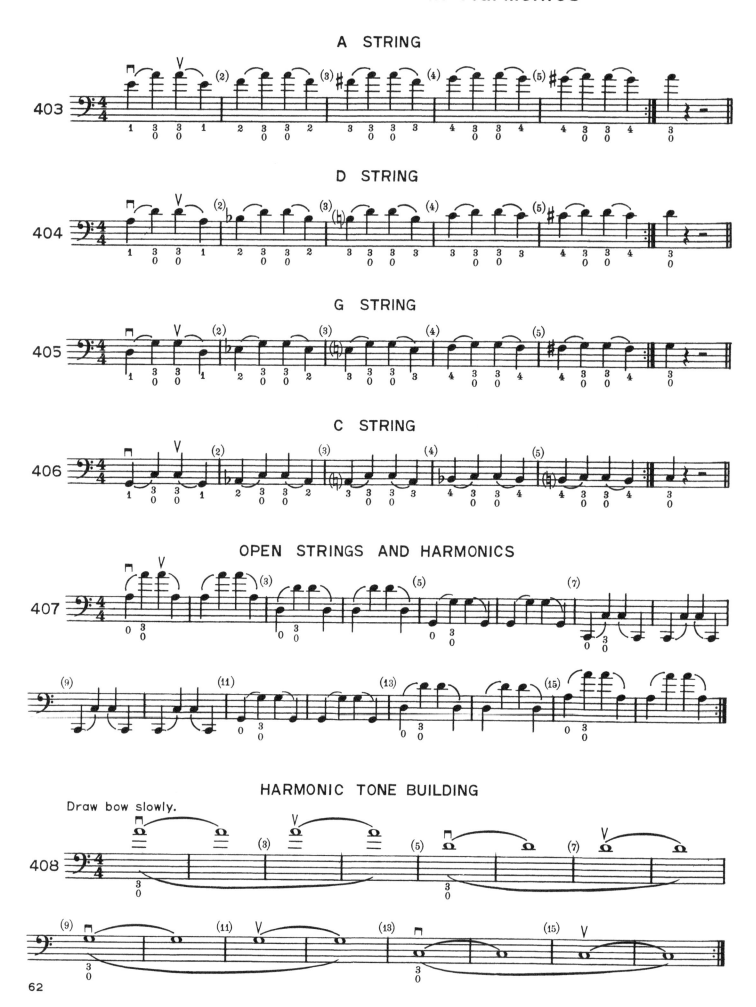

Scales Employing Four Positions

SCALE OF F MAJOR

SCALE OF E MAJOR

Position Etudes

Selected from the works of Lee, Werner and Kummer

Etude No. 1 in C

LEE

Etude No. 2 in C

LEE

Etude in G

LEE

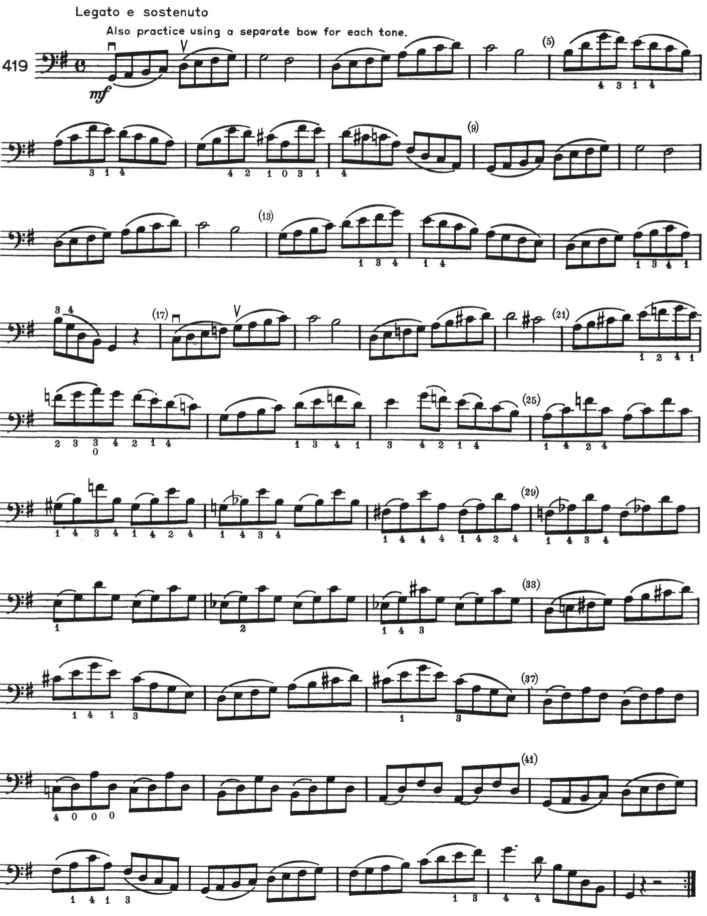

Etude in B♭

LEE

Etude in A

LEE

Advanced Etude in the Second Position

WERNER

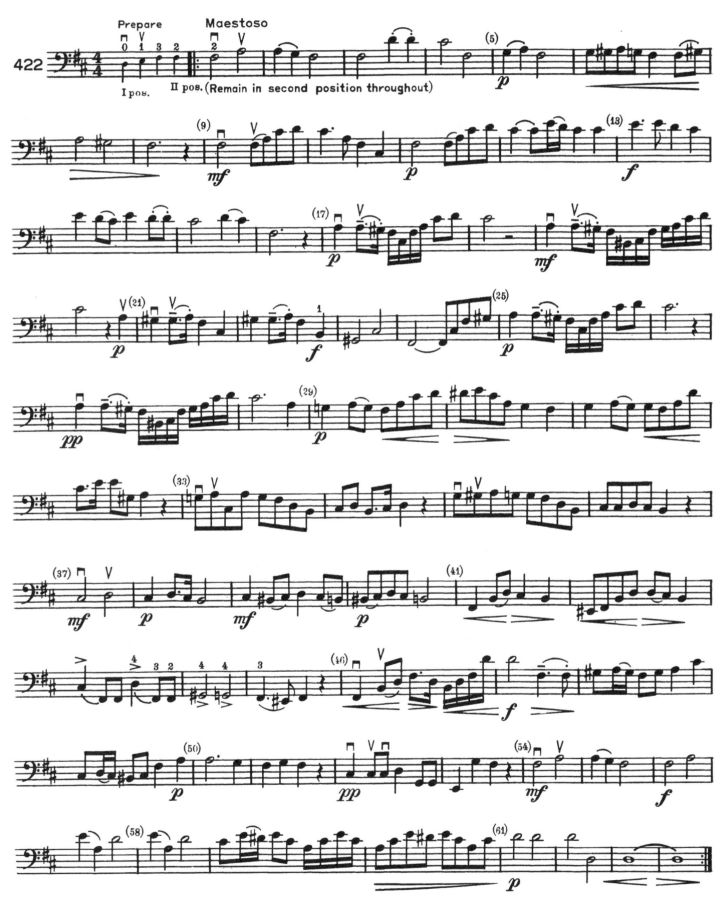

Advanced Etude in the First, Third and Fourth Positions

WERNER

Chromatic Caprice
(Duet)

KUMMER